DEC 1 5 2017

How Is a Sweater Made?

by Grace Hansen

Abdo
HOW IS IT MADE?
Kids

abdopublishing.com

Published by Abdo Kids, a division of ABDO, P.O. Box 398166, Minneapolis, Minnesota 55439.

Copyright © 2018 by Abdo Consulting Group, Inc. International copyrights reserved in all countries. No part of this book may be reproduced in any form without written permission from the publisher.

Printed in the United States of America, North Mankato, Minnesota.

052017

092017

 THIS BOOK CONTAINS RECYCLED MATERIALS

Photo Credits: Getty Images, iStock, Shutterstock

Production Contributors: Teddy Borth, Jennie Forsberg, Grace Hansen

Design Contributors: Dorothy Toth, Laura Mitchell

Publisher's Cataloging in Publication Data

Names: Hansen, Grace, author.

Title: How is a sweater made? / by Grace Hansen.

Description: Minneapolis, Minnesota : Abdo Kids, 2018 | Series: How is it made? | Includes bibliographical references and index.

Identifiers: LCCN 2016962397 | ISBN 9781532100444 (lib. bdg.) | ISBN 9781532101137 (ebook) | ISBN 9781532101687 (Read-to-me ebook)

Subjects: LCSH: Sweaters--Juvenile literature. | Yarn--Juvenile literature.

Classification: DDC 687/.146--dc23

LC record available at http://lccn.loc.gov/2016962397

Table of Contents

Making Sweaters

Sweaters can be made from many different materials. Two popular materials are cotton and wool.

4

Cotton

Cotton is a plant. It grows in fields. It is **harvested** each year. The time of year depends on where the field is located.

7

Seeds and cotton are separated from the **bolls**. The seed cotton is then sent to a **cotton gin**. It is dried and cleaned. The seeds are separated from the cotton.

Cotton is sent to a **textile mill**. Here, it is cleaned again, brushed, spun, and woven into yarn. Machines called looms weave the yarn into a product that can be made into clothing.

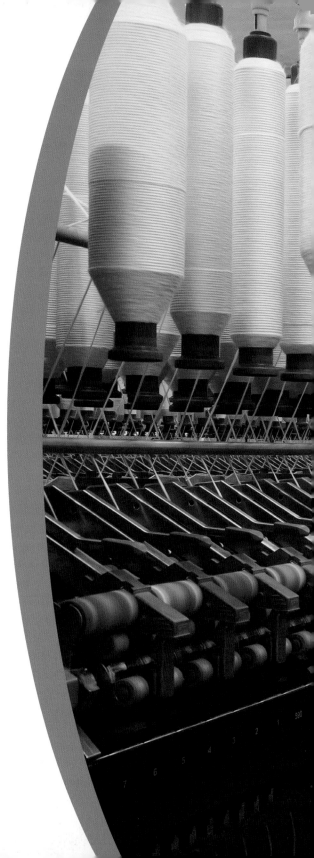

11

Wool

Wool comes from sheep.
Sheep grow thick wool
coats each year. These
keep them warm in the winter.

At the end of winter, sheep are sheared. This happens just before they would shed naturally.

The wool is then cleaned with soap and water, and combed. Combing the wool makes it softer. Then the wool is dyed.

Wool is then spun into yarn. Multiple strands are twisted together. This makes a strong finished product.

19

The Finished Product

Some sweaters are knitted by hand. But machines make most sweaters.